MONEY EQUATION:
How to save more money and retire RICH

The purpose of this eBook is to educate you about the two sides in the money equation. It focuses on the expenses side of the equation and help you find ways of cutting down cost so that you can have more money in your bank account at the end of each month. The strategy of growing wealth is to ensure that your monthly expenses is always lower than your monthly income and you must ensure that you constantly invest the excess to generate good returns for you. This eBook will show you how to painlessly cut down your monthly expenses, save more money, and how you can invest your savings so that you can achieve financial freedom. The book is divided into three parts;

1. How to reduce your living expenses
2. How to achieve financial prosperity.
3. How to make your money work for you.

MONEY EQUATION

- **INCOME – EXPENSES = SAVINGS**
- **FINANCIAL PROPERITY = INCOME > EXPENSES**
- **DEBT = EXPENSES > INCOME**
- **PAYCHECK TO PAYCHECK (RAT RACE) = INCOME = EXPENSES**

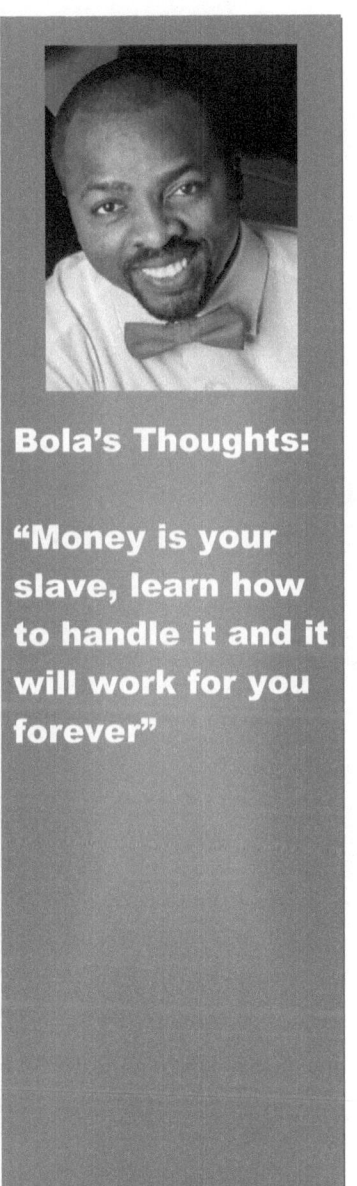

Bola's Thoughts:

"Money is your slave, learn how to handle it and it will work for you forever"

Introduction

The subject of money is a universal one. Everyone speaks the money language but only a few truly understand the language that money speaks. People all over the world interact with money, but they don't know how to properly handle it. People work hard every day of their lives to earn money, but they don't know how to make their money work for them in return. Money aid in ensuring that we meet our needs as human beings. You need money to buy food to eat, clothes to cover your body, get a house to provide roof over your head, and to meet with most of your other needs and wants. Nowadays, many people in order to earn more money, have chosen to work so many hours just to ensure that they can make more money at the end of each month to cover their living expenses. The major issue that most people confront is that their income is not sufficient to cover all their monthly commitment and to cover the shortfall, most people resort to using credit cards thereby going into debt. There are other seemingly rich people that still perpetuate in debt, living pay check to paycheck and they do not know what to do or steps to take that will get them out of the rat race.

To win with your money, you need to understand the money equation and learn how you can use the equation to create a life of financial prosperity. There are two sides in the equation of money management. There is incoming side which covers all the money you earn either inform of salary, wages, royalties, rental income, dividends, and earnings from business investment. The other side of the equation is the outgoing side, which deals with the money you spend. And this includes but not limited to money you spend on food, clothing, housing, fun activities and so on. The secret to winning with your money is to make sure that your outgoing is always less than your incoming. That way, you will have surplus, and you can invest and make money work for you.

PART 1:

15 WAYS TO REDUCE YOUR MONTHLY EXPENSES

Cutting down cost and being able to save money is what everyone desires irrespective of their financial status. It will be unusual to find someone willing to pay more for an item when they can get the exact same item with the same quality and features for a lesser price. It is even stranger to find someone just throwing money out or burning their money just because they are so rich. So, whether you are wealthy, in the middle class, or poor, you want to ensure you are getting the biggest bang for your buck. So, the purpose of this section is to share awesome and easy tricks that will help you reduce your living expenses thereby saving more money at the end of every month.

Here are some awesome ideas that will allow you to stretch your dollar further.

1. **Reduce your bills:** The bills you pay on a monthly basis is on the outgoing side of your financial equation. Cutting down your monthly bills will ensure that you can keep more money in your pocket. Cutting down does not always have to be painful, making some conscious decision and becoming more responsible can help you reduce your bills and therefore set you up on the path of financial prosperity. Making choices to reduce your monthly bills will help improve your financial well-being and give you more satisfaction. In America we pay all sorts of bills at the end of the month, some of the bills includes; Insurance, Phone bills, Utility bills and so on. For most families in America today, after paying all their bills, they are left with nothing to save and enjoy, and that is why people work many hours to make more money. Enough of the rat race, here are some ideas that will help you save on your monthly bills. These are less painful choices that can help save about $100 each month on average.

- **Insurance:** The insurance market place especially on the auto and homeowner side is very competitive. You are the boss here, and you need to make the insurance companies compete for your business. Just like Geico slogan, "fifteen minutes could save you fifteen percent or more on your insurance premium." Spending a little time in front of your computer could save you hundreds of dollars each year on your insurance premium. Here is what you should do immediately. Go to "Nerdwallet" website to compare rates: https://www.nerdwallet.com/insurance/compare-car-insurance-rates. For your homeowner insurance, I want you to head to "Quote wizard" to get the best rates. https://quotewizard.com/home-insurance. With this approach, you can easily save on average about $20 on your monthly insurance premium.

- **Electricity:** An average family spends $1400 every year on electricity. You can achieve a saving of about $10 each month on your electricity bills. You should use the "Power2switch" website to compare rates. You can read the terms, cancellation policies of each providers on the website before you make your choice. Here is their website: https://power2switch.com/ If you live in the great state of Texas, power to choose (http://powertochoose.org/en-us) website works pretty well. All you need to do is to put your zip code and they will list all the electricity providers around you. I recently used this service, and when I put my zip code, it turned up with over 150 providers that can supply electricity to my house. Why would I want to pay 11c per kwh for electricity when I can get it for 8.2c per kwh? It's the same electricity, my appliances work just fine irrespective of the provider.

- **Internet and Cables:** The average cable TV and internet package in the US is about $150. Many people are subscribed to TV packages that they do not watch or need. These TV packages are bundled with hundreds of channels just so that the TV companies can charge you more money. It is almost impossible to have a program that you like to watch on all the of the channels that they bundled together for you. If you are really a TV addict, maybe you will typically watch 20 to 30 channels at most. Why pay for what you don't use? You can make significant savings by cutting your cable TV subscriptions and going for the streaming services instead. Sling TV, DIRECTV now, Hulu, and YouTube offer several TV packages at lower cost. You can also watch on demand, unlimited movies on Amazon Primenow, Netflix at a very cheap cost. You can easily save over $40 each month by making the switch

- **Phone bills:** According to a study from CouponCabin.com, 46 percent of cell phone owners have a bill of at least $100 per month. The big 3 "AT&T, Verizon, and Tmobile" are mostly on the higher end of the cost especially if you use the unlimited data, talk, and text plan. If you're looking to save money on your phone bill this year, consider going for the low-cost, no-contract options before changing your provider. There is no real need to worry about coverage, either, as many of the low-cost options use the same networks as the larger providers and therefore you will not be sacrificing coverage for price. You should also determine if you need the unlimited plans to begin with. If you go to the low-cost provider, you can save an average of about $30 each month.

⬛ **Total Monthly Savings on Bill Management: $100 to $150 or more.**
⬛ **Total Yearly Savings: $1,200 to $1,800 or more.**

Idea #2

2. **Take lunch to work:** Packing your lunch to work can save you hundreds of dollars every year. The cost of going out for lunch varies depending on the choice you are making – you may spend as low as $5 if you go the fast food route, or as high as $20 if you decide to go to a restaurant. Just for the sake of being conservative, if you eat McDonald Burger every day for five days of the working week, you will spend $25 each week and that translates to $100 per month. You can prepare varieties of good meal at home that will last you a whole week for less than $50. You can save $50 every month if you decide to take you lunch to work. Brown bagging does not only help you to cut down cost, but it also ensures that you are eating healthy. You will also be saving money on gas as you drive to and from the lunch spot. I am not advocating that you should bring lunch to work 100% of the time, but if you are ever going to eat out, look for online deals at https://www.restaurant.com/ you may be able to save up to 40% of the original cost. You can also achieve more savings by making sure you eat breakfast at home before setting out to work every morning. This is quite easy to do with varieties of choices at your disposal. You can take oatmeal, cereal, fruits, toast, yoghurt, waffles, and so on. These foods are quick and easy to prepare. My goal is to help you to maximize your income, reduce your expenses as much as possible so that you can have more savings at the end of every month, one easy way to do this is to take your lunch to work. Enjoy your homemade meal and put more money in your pocket.

- **Total Monthly Savings on Lunch: $100 to $250 or more.**
- **Total Yearly Savings: $1,200 to $3,000 or more.**

Idea #3

coffee

3. **Make your own coffee:** Americans love coffee. As a matter of fact, most people are now addicted to coffee. I have couple of friends that confessed that they are not 100 percent at alert if they have not taken their morning coffee. Do you know that an average American worker spends about $15 a week on coffee? Depending on the store you go, whether it is a mom-and-pop store, Starbucks or Dunkin Donuts, you can expect to shell out a minimum of $3 per visit. Your coffee fanfare can cost you about $1,000 per year. It is okay to love coffee, but your wallet shouldn't have to suffer the pain of your splurge. You can enjoy your coffee in a cheaper way. You should consider brewing your coffee at home, this way you can save about 50% on coffee. If your employer provides coffee at the workplace, ditch the store-bought coffee and rely on your employer to supply your morning coffee need, see it as one of the perks that comes with working with the company. You can also bring your coffee machine to the office if your company does not provide coffee. The debate around whether coffee is healthy or not is still brewing, you can consider reducing your coffee intake and instead drink more water.

- Total Monthly Savings on Breakfast: $50 to $80 or more
- Total Yearly Savings: $600 to $960 or more

Idea #4

4. **<u>Consider DIY:</u>** Taking out time to get some of home maintenance and repair work done by yourself can save you thousands of dollars each year. For example, you can save about $50 on average each month by mowing your lawn yourself, $30 each month by cutting your hair yourself, $40 each month by getting your nails done at home, $50 for doing your laundry at home, and you can save $25 whenever you change the oil in your car by yourself. You can save a lot more if you decide to perform repair work by yourself at home. For example, I had to fix my garage door by myself last summer. The garage door often gets stuck or open involuntarily. All I googled the make and model and I got some troubleshooting guide that helped fix it. I also researched for it on YouTube and I was able to watch some videos on the step-by-step instructions on how to fix the garage door. I was able to save about $100 by doing this myself. A friend of mine recently moved to a new house and he used the DIY approach to paint his house. This saved couple of hundred bucks in the process.

There are other DIY projects that you can undertake at home to achieve more savings, for example, you can make your homemade laundry detergent, deodorant, and hair conditioner. The good news here is that there are lots of DIY bloggers that can help guide you in case you are unfamiliar with what you need to do in order to complete the repair work. You will not be an expert the first time you try this, but with constant practice, you will develop more knowledge and competence in carrying out DIY projects around your house. The satisfaction and fulfillment that comes with doing stuffs yourself far outweigh the savings you achieved in the process. Try DIY, you will learn and save money in the process.

- **Total Monthly Savings with DIY: $100 to $200 or more**
- **Total Yearly Savings: $1,200 to $2,400 or more**

Idea #5

5. **Cancel your gym membership:** I'm a fitness enthusiast. I enjoy using the treadmill and lifting weight, but I have access to free gym in my neighborhood. I was a member of the LA Fitness for many years and I was spending $35 each month to keep my membership at the club. Yes, they have a lot more equipment than my community gym, but I was not using more than 3 different machines when I was a member of the gym. Why would I continue to pay $35 each month on gym that I only use three times a week when I can do just the same exercise for free? To me, goodbye to LA fitness means more money in my pocket. So, my recommendation is that you should cancel your gym membership immediately if you have access to gym in your neighborhood. If you struggle to go to the gym as a result of work or time constraint, it is time to cancel the membership. If you do not have a community fitness center, you can build your own home gym, it is quite easy to do. Get on YouTube and you will be able to watch exercise training videos, exercise tutorials are also available on Pinterest. If you love the outdoor, please hit the park and enjoy natural light and breeze as you run down the trail, you can do this at no cost to you. Let's put your gym membership fees back into your bank account and find a good investment that will ensure that your money works for you.

- **Total Monthly Savings on Gym Membership Cancellation: $35 to $75 or more**

- **Total Yearly Savings: $420 to $900 or more**

Idea #6

6. **Use rewards and coupons:** Clipping coupons take extreme plans and determination. You have to be motivated and stay committed before you can see results. If you are all in on using coupons and reward points to get discounts on your purchase, you will be able to save thousands of dollars every year. I personally do not like using coupons, but from my discussion with people that do use them, I think it can be beneficial if you are looking to cut down on cost. Most people are familiar with coupons in newspapers, but there are digital coupons that you can download online as well. You can use coupons on varieties of products such as groceries, vehicle oil change, drug store and so on. There are several loyalty programs available that companies use to attract more customers, joining those loyalty programs will automatically qualify you for special discounts on your purchases. Filling out surveys can also help you to get coupons that you can apply to get some rewards. My local pizza chain Marco's pizza typically gives out "cheezy bread" whenever a customer fills out their survey. I love frozen yogurt, and I take advantage of Tutti Frutti rewards program to get some discount on my yogurt. For every $50 that I spend on yogurt, they give me $5 in return towards the next purchase. In terms of clipping coupons, there is no other website that offers varieties of options like coupons.com. They have coupons on varieties of products such as chewing gum, body cream, chocolate, groceries items, retail items, and computer equipment. I am sure you will find something useful to you if you get on their website. I love and utilize royalty reward as well. You can achieve a lot of savings using this perk. Some few years back, I took a trip to London and I was able to stay in one of Marriott Hotel for free for a week by simply tapping into my reward points. A buddy of mine uses his airline reward points to book a trip to Hawaii for vacation last summer. If you are the type that use credit card, there are some credit cards that offers customer loyalty points and you can redeem your points as cash or other gift items. Rewards and coupons can be a way of earning some passive income, you just have to understand the requirements before you can take the full benefits.

- **Total Monthly Savings on Coupons/Loyalty rewards: $35 to $75 or more.**
- **Total Yearly Savings: $420 to $900 or more.**

Idea #7

7. **Be conservative:** This is not in any way referring to your political views, but your spending behavior. Are you the type that splurge on things you don't really need in order to impress the people that don't really care about you? If so, you need to make changes and start living within your means. Don't try to keep up with the Joneses, don't buy a new car every four year because your neighbors are driving the latest car on the lot. Don't buy a new iPhone every time Apple rolled out their latest version. You are making Apple and its executive richer and denying yourself the opportunity to build wealth by doing so. Conserve electricity at home by turning off power when you are away and using energy efficient appliance. Cut down energy leaks in your house, close blinds or shades during the day. Use programmable thermostat to control the temperature in your house and when you are away you can adjust the temperature about two to three degrees higher than when you are in during the summer season or lower during the winter. Look to buy items when they are on sale and buy clothes off season. For example, you will get some great discount if you buy your winter jacket immediately after winter than when you buy it during the peak of the cold weather. I have a friend that bought the Christmas decoration items in 2016 around January when virtually many people are already in the process of packing up their decorations. Yes, he was unable to decorate his house in 2016, but he got the items on sales at almost 40% discount, and he was able to join the bandwagon of home decoration in 2017. This is also a lesson in delayed gratification. Are you in the process of buying something new? Is it urgent? Can you wait a little bit more? If you can wait, then go ahead and wait, you may end up realizing that you do not need the item in the first place, thereby saving you from unnecessary expenses.

- Estimated Monthly Savings on being conservative: $20 to $30 or more
- Estimated Yearly Savings: $240 to $360 or more

Idea #8

8. **Drink more water:** Water is almost a free commodity. I know we all pay water bills, but when compared with other kind of drinks the amount you spend on water is minuscule. If you can drink more water and ditch most other types of drinks such as juice, tea, coffee, soda, or alcoholic beverages, you will be able to put more money back in your pocket. Apart from the cost benefits that comes with drinking more water, you will also derive the health benefits of water because it will help flush out dangerous toxins out of your body, it helps in boosting your brain power and also in stimulating your digestive system. Put more money in your pocket and stay healthy by drinking more water.

- Estimated Monthly Savings on drinking more water: $10 to $20 or more.
- Estimated Yearly Savings: $120 to $240 or more

Idea #9

9. **Do a price comparison**: Before you make that purchase, take a pause and take a moment to do a price comparison. Several tools and websites are available that can help you make the most of your money. Again, why would anyone want to spend more money on a piece of an item if they can get the exact same item with the same quality at a lower price? Using the price comparison tool can help you save money on all your purchases. Some of the website that I use for price comparison includes: Shopzilla, PriceGrabber, Google Shopping, and Pronto. Using the price comparison websites will put you in bargain-hunting mode, whereby you can know the prices from various retailers right from the comfort of your house. You do not have to go out or visit ten different websites before you can compare prices and make decision on how and where to spend your money. Retailers also get into price wars in order to have a cut at your hard-earned money. There are many times when companies like Best Buy, Walmart, or Target do price match on some of their products in order to win your business. The strategy to use here is to show them a proof that the item you are about to buy is available cheaper elsewhere. For example, when next you go to Walmart to buy an item, you can quickly check the price of the item on Target or Amazon. If they are cheaper on those websites, and if there is a price match offer on the item, Walmart will be willing to match the price for you. That way you can get discounts on the item without needing to drive around to Target. It is all about putting more money in your pocket.

- Estimated Monthly Savings on being conservative: $20 to $40 or more
- Estimated Yearly Savings: $240 to $480 or more

Idea #10

10. **Have a shopping list:** It is always a good practice to have a shopping list before embarking on any shopping expedition. If you don't have the list of what you plan to buy, there is a high chance that you will buy items that are not necessary or important to you. You will basically be an impulse buyer without your shopping list. I am not big on shopping, but in the past whenever I go out to buy items, I always have a mental list of what I needed. I realized that on most occasion, I will end up buying other items that I might have wanted in the past but that are no longer important to me. I learnt this lesson and I started going out with my shopping list and this has helped me to keep to my budget and also control my expenses. There is no benefit to having a shopping list if you are not going to stick with it, so the most important thing about having your shopping list is to make sure that you follow your list. You need to have the right discipline to make sure you honor your commitment by only buying things that are in your list, you can always wait for another day to buy other non-critical items. Your shopping list will help you to prioritize your spending, put you in control of expenses and help ensure that you are not over spending your money.

- **Estimated Monthly Savings on being conservative: $20 to $40 or more.**
- **Estimated Yearly Savings: $240 to $480 or more.**

Idea #11

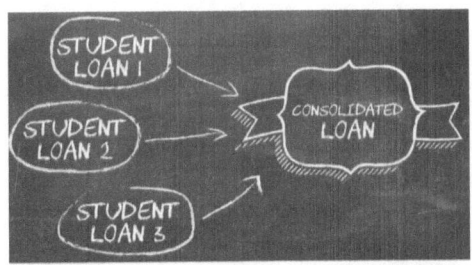

11. **Consolidate and refinance your student loans:** Student loans is a menace in America. An average graduate owes about $30,000 in student loan debt with an average monthly payment of about $250. I once had some student loan myself, and I had to consolidate and refinance all my student loans. The interest rate on my student loan debt went from around 8.5% to less than 6% as a result, thereby saving me an average of $100 each month in interest payment. I applied the savings on the interest towards the principal and I was able to pay off my student loans quicker. The Fed is gradually raising interest rate, but you can still refinance your student loan to take advantage of the current low interest rate in the country. I will recommend SOFI as the go to company for student loan refinancing. If you are able to make extra payment on the principal, you should definitely consider it because that strategy will help you to quickly pay off your student loans.

- Total Monthly Savings on refinancing student loans: $100 to $150 or more
- Total Yearly Savings: $1,200 to $1,500 or more

Idea #12

12. **Ditch all forms of debt:** Debt is a huge hinderance in your journey to financial freedom. It will make a big impact in your retirement portfolio if you can put the interests you pay on your recurring debt towards your retirement account. According to a report on CNBC.com, the average American has a credit card balance of $6,375. At about 16% annual interest rate on credit card, you are paying a monthly interest of about $80 if you carry a balance of $6,000 on your credit card. In the same way, the average monthly payment for a new vehicle is slightly over $500, while the payment on a used car is about $350. Imagine what you could do with your money if you have no monthly payment on credit card or auto loan. If you already have these debts, you need to reassess and take decisions on how to eliminate them. I recommend the following steps:

a. *Stop accumulating more debt:* Budget is a powerful tool that you can use to tell your money where to go. Ensure you set up a budget, if you are unable to meet all your needs and wants on any particular month, it's okay to wait till the following month as long as you are able to: Eat, pay your rent/mortgage, pay your bills, and pay your transportation to and from work. You will need to prioritize all other expenses and only pay for what you can cover each month. The other thing you could do is to find a job that will pay more or take on extra work.

b. *Sell your car:* If you are driving those expensive cars with monthly payments that takes a large percentage of your income, then you should consider selling the car and see if you can buy a cheaper car with cash or lower monthly payment.

c. *Negotiate with your banker:* Banks make a lot of money charging you interests on your credit card, auto loan and any debt you owe them. Stop making the banks richer and put more of your money back in your pocket by asking for lower interest rates from the banks.

- **Estimated Monthly Savings on living with no debt: $100 to $500 or more.**

- **Estimated Yearly Savings: $1,200 to $6,000 or more**

Idea #13

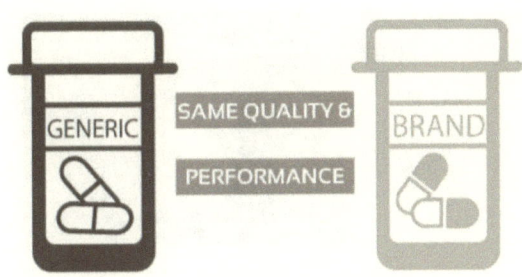

13. **Go generic:** Put more money in your pocket by buying generic items and ditch the name brand. Whether it is about buying cough syrup, cereals, cookies, batteries, or clothes, product with the brand name recognition tend to be more expensive than their generic counterparts. In most of these cases higher prices do not always mean better quality. Many stores now offer store brands in order to compete with the popular brand names. For example, Walmart's store brand – "Great value" has manufactured several products such as bath tissue, kitchen towels, and cereals, to compete with manufacturers like Charmin, Dixie, and General Mills. CVS and Walgreen have their branded aspirin to compete with Johnson & Johnson the maker of Tylenol. There is no reason to spend more money buying brand names, the generic counterparts are identical to the name brands in many ways in terms of ingredients used in the products. Brand names are not better quality, go generic and put more money in your pocket. Here is a list of some products you should consider switching to generic immediately"

   I. Medications
   II. Milk
   III. Baby Formula
   IV. Paper plates and aluminum foil
   V. Water
   VI. Detergents
   VII. Cereal
   VIII. Diapers
   IX. Soda
   X. Personal care products

- **Estimated Monthly Savings on buying generic items: $10 to $20 or more.**

- **Estimated Yearly Savings: $120 to $240 or more**

Idea #14

14. **Cancel unused subscriptions:** I have amazon prime video subscription, Netflix, Showtime, and Hulu. I hardly watch programs on all the three platforms. My prime video subscription was as an add on to my Amazon prime membership. I subscribed to showtime because I wanted to watch the homeland series. So, I had four video subscription and I only watch one or two. I cancel my Showtime and Hulu subscriptions saving about $17 each month. I love reading magazines especially on business topics. I'm subscribed to Inc, Entrepreneur, Money, Fortune, and Forbes magazines. It became extremely difficult for me to keep up and stay current on my magazine subscriptions. I cancelled my subscriptions from two of the magazines and I am now able to keep up with the rest. Do you have any unused subscriptions? Try and cancel the ones you don't use regularly so that you can put more money back into your pocket. In my own case, months will go by without even turning on Hulu or Showtime, so I did the reasonable thing, I cancelled my subscription with these companies. Are you ready to save more money? Cancel your unused membership or subscriptions for one month. If you miss it or if you think it's very important for you, you can go back and subscribe again, otherwise keep the extra money in your pocket.

- **Estimated Monthly Savings on canceling unused subscriptions: $10 to $15 or more**
- **Estimated Yearly Savings: $120 to $180 or more**

Idea #15

15. **Switch to term life insurance:** The term life and whole life insurance are two common life insurance products being sold by insurance companies. Typically, the premium you pay on the whole life insurance is a lot higher than the premium on the term life insurance. The purpose of a life insurance is to replace your income for your family if you die. This is very useful as long as you have people that depend on your income. You can save a lot by switching from whole life insurance to term life insurance. The Term life insurance provides coverage for a specific period of time (typically 20–30 years). The whole life on the other hand provides coverage throughout your entire life. The premium on these two insurance products is where the biggest difference lies. A typical healthy 30-year-old man may be charged a premium of about $25 per month on a 20-year term life insurance with coverage of $500,000, same coverage for a whole life may be about $200. Switch to a term life insurance and save the difference and put the extra back into your account.

- **Estimated Monthly Savings on switching to term life insurance: $100 to $250 or more**

- **Estimated Yearly Savings: $1,200 to $3,000 or more**

If saving money and getting to keep more of your money is your goal, then any of the above approach should work for you. You can save as little as $1,200 to as much as $3,000 every year using this less painful options. You can put yourself in a better position by managing your expenses, making sure that your expenses are less than your income from month to month. If you constantly ensure that you are in control of your spending, you will be able to keep more of your money, and if you invest the excess for a long haul, you will be able to add more money to your retirement portfolio. The ideas shared so far are not in anyway exhaustive, there are hundreds of other ideas that you can explore to save more money. The goal of this section is to motivate you to always find ways of reducing your living expenses.

PART 2:

7 STEPS TO ACHIEVE FINANCIAL PROSPERITY

Now that you have taken the appropriate steps to reduce your monthly expenses, I want to help you save those extra money to ensure that you are in a position to achieve financial prosperity. The easiest path to financial freedom is to have money work for you and generate passive income that will one day replace your current income.

Have you ever wondered why the rich get richer, the poor get poorer, with the middle class in constant rat race? Why is it that the top 1% makes much more than the next 90% of the population combined? How did Jeff Bezos amass over $100 billion? The goal of this section is to teach you how to save money and use the savings to earn more money. You will be able to increase your financial net worth by following the steps highlighted in this section.

A lot of us know that we ought to save, invest, and spend money, but what most people do not know is that there is a simple step that they can follow to achieve financial prosperity. Many people try to save what is left after spending their money, and several studies have shown that this is not a winning strategy. To win with money, you must tell your money where to go at the end of each month when you get your pay check. If you do this consistently over many years, you can achieve financial freedom and attain a state where you don't have to get all stressed up about money.

Below are the seven principles of financial prosperity for anyone looking to achieve financial independence.

<u>SEVEN PRINCIPLES OF FINANCIAL PROSPERITY</u>

1. <u>*Pay yourself first:*</u> Take one-tenth of what you bring in and save it for the future. You must decide that a part of all you earned is for you to keep. No one can accumulate wealth without saving part of what they earn. Now depending on your situation, 10% may not be possible, but don't let that stop you from paying yourself first. You work hard, paying yourself first is a way of rewarding yourself and it will help you to learn how to save money. The challenge for most people here is how can they save one-tenth of their income when the entire income is not even sufficient to pay for their living expenses? If 10% is extremely difficult for you, then you can start with 1%, the idea is that you must keep something at the end of each month. You must however have a goal to increase your monthly savings as time goes by. The money you are using to pay yourself is what you will use to start creating extra income for yourself and building your wealth.

2. *Tell your money where to go:* Most people work very hard to earn their income, but they do not work as hard to tell their money where to go at the end of each month. Budgeting is an essential tool that will help you to take control of your money and without this tool, they become impulsive and spend their hard-earned money carelessly. Budgeting is about being discipline, but unfortunately most people do not enjoy the budgeting process and that is why many get into debt. Budgeting will help you allocate your God's giving resources appropriately, so you don't end up wondering where your money went at the end of the month. There are so many budgeting apps out there that you can use to manage your finances. I personally use Mint to plan my expenses for each month, but there are other budgeting apps that you can use. You can as well use the old and tested method of using excel spreadsheet to manage your finances. Just make sure that what is going out each month does not exceed what is coming in and you keep to your commitment as planned in the budget.

3. *Control your expenses*: In a world of instant gratification, most people want whatever they want right now without necessarily given a good thought to how they will pay for it. We have millions of people living in homes they cannot afford, driving cars on credit, and going on vacation courtesy of Master and Visa credit card. If you want to achieve financial prosperity, then you need to know how to wait for some of those wants in your life. You should stop spending what you do not have by controlling your expenses. If you continue to live within your means, after so many years, you will see the results as you will start accumulating surpluses. Don't buy frivolous things even if you have enough money to pay for them. Instead, make sure that you can continue to save one-tenth of what you bring in. Controlling your expenditures enable you to make good use of the money you have left over after you have paid yourself first.

4. *Get out of debt:* Debt is a disease and it can rob you of your peace if you don't attack and defeat it. To win with your finances, you need to ensure that you don't get into debt, and if you are already in some form of debt, you need to work hard and get out immediately. You should make it a priority to get out of debt, you should work hard by taking on extra jobs, deliver pizza, drive Uber, don't go to eat out in a restaurant, sell unnecessary stuffs to raise money, and you go on rice and beans, beans and rice nutritional plan. The goal is to make sure you quickly pay off your debt so that you can stop being a slave to the lenders. Here is a proven strategy to paying off your debt. If you have more than one, list them from smallest to largest and start attacking from the least one until all the debts are paid off. Debt is a burden that will keep you in constant bondage and you must do everything you can to ensure you get out of it. Debt is an obligation to the past that will deny you of opportunities to invest in your future.

5. *Make your money work for you:* Once you start to build up some savings, invest that money so that it will make more money for you. There are many investment vehicles that can be used to make your money work for you. You should never invest in anything you do not completely understand. There are many ways we can invest our money such as stock markets, real estate, businesses, and so on. For example, in the United States, you can invest in mutual funds with long track record of generating solid returns and tap into the benefits of compound interest. The way to make your money work for you is through re-investment of interest or income you are generating from your investments. If you invest your money in the stock market for example, don't spend the quarterly dividends that you collect from your investment, you should rather reinvest it so that it will also work for you. The same analogy applies to the rent that you collect from real estate investment, you should save it to buy more properties that will generate more income for you. Money is your

slave by learning how to make it work for you and handle it properly, it will keep producing extra income for you.

6. *Protect your money from loss:* Now that you have developed the habit of saving money, the next thing to learn is how to protect your money from loss. We must first secure small amounts and learn to protect them before God can entrust us with larger amount. The first principle of investment is security of the principal. Don't take unnecessary risk if you are not sure that your money will be protected. Don't invest in get rich quick scheme. If something is too good to be true, then it is too good to be true. To invest and generate returns takes time, and you need to do your homework and research before you put your money into any form of investment. Make sure you have some knowledge and some comfort level before you take the plunge, and you should also have a long-term focus to allow proper time for your investments to start generating returns to you. More money will naturally come to a cautious owner who invests it under the advice of experts in financial management. You may need to consult a financial manager to help you set up how to account portfolio so that it can become an income generating machine. Money will slip away from the man who invests carelessly in business or purposes that he is not familiar with.

7. *Increase your ability to earn:* The best way we can increase our earning is by investing in ourselves. We can do that by continually learning and striving to develop ourselves. Work hard, look for opportunities, and educate yourself. Today, a college education is one of the best investments you can make; I'm not saying that it's a requirement to be successful, but it opens the door to greater possibilities. You should aim for continuous improvements and look for opportunities that will make you get better at what you do. You must have a growth mindset and seek for opportunities that will challenge and help you to stretch beyond your comfort zone. By taking up more responsibilities in your organization, you are telling your boss that you want to grow and learn more, and promotions typically comes with more income.

PART 3:

HOW TO MAKE YOUR MONEY WORK FOR YOU

An average person that diligently followed the recommendations in part 1 can save as low as $100 and up to as much as $500 per month. There are fifteen recommendations and the more of them that you can implement the higher the savings that you will be able to make at the end of each month.

There are many people that still struggle about where to put their money so that they can generate good returns. In the United States, several studies have shown that long term investing and capitalizing on the benefits of compound interest can help you retire rich if you stay focused. There are several tools such as 401K plan, ROTH investments, and Real Estates investing that provides tax incentives for people that set aside a proportion of their income for investment purposes. Furthermore, using the dollar cost average concept; whereby you invest certain amount at a particular date of each month into an investment vehicle regardless of what is occurring in the market is a good strategy for you to adopt to reap the full benefits of the market. That means you continue to invest whether the market is up or down. This concept coupled with having a long-term horizon for investing is a winning strategy.

For example, in a recent publication, the average number of 401K millionaires reached a peak of 157,000 people. These are people that have been able to amass at least a million dollar in their investment portfolio. These people stayed the course during the bull and the bear market, they kept investing every month and the results manifested in the retirement portfolio. Do not try to time the market, no one can truly predict the market, and if your strategy is to wait for a buying opportunity, you may as well miss the train and the capital gains that you could have earned if you had invested. If you are just starting out in your career, try and contribute the maximum you can to your retirement account. Most employers provide the benefits of matching certain percentage of your contributions. For example, some companies will match your contribution dollar for dollar up to certain amount that you put in your retirement account. Make sure you take full advantage of your employer 401K plan and after many years of setting money aside towards your retirement, you will start seeing results.

The ultimate point to note is that you need to put your money in an investment vehicle that will yield good returns for you. I am not a big fan of investing in individual stock, although some of them have performed very well over the past decades yet I consider putting money in a single stock as a big risk that I cannot afford to take. It is the proverbial equivalent of putting all your eggs in one basket. My recommendation is to find mutual funds with long track record of tracking or over-performing the market. The mutual fund is a basket of stocks from different companies, some can contain as many as 500 companies. It is possible that a few of the companies in the fund may not perform very well in a particular year, this will not necessarily affect the overall fund because other stocks in the basket are performing very well. This way, you are able to diversify your risks and avoid the possibility of losing all your money if you had invested in single stocks.

Based on the history of the market in the United States, every so often, the market sometimes self-correct itself, whereby there may be a plunge in the market with lots of companies' stocks on sale. Rather than panicking and selling your investment, this is an opportunity for you to double down and put in more money so that you can make more money when the market eventually recovers. It always will.

See some charts below that explains how you much your money will be worth after certain number of years. I did the chart based on $100 or $500 monthly contribution with an annual return of 10% and 12%.

1. Based on Age
2. Based on Amount

Age	No of yrs	$500 every month @ 12% ROI	$500 every month @ 10% ROI
25	40	$5,154,854	$2,921,111
30	35	$2,900,779	$1,788,761
35	30	$1,621,756	$1,085,661
40	25	$896,004	$649,091
45	20	$484,192	$378,015
50	15	$250,520	$209,698
55	10	$117,927	$105,187

Table 1: Saving $500 every month at ROI 10% and 12%.

Age	No of yrs	$100 Monthly saving @ 12% ROI	$100 Monthly saving @ 10% ROI
25	40	$1,030,971	$584,222
30	35	$580,156	$357,752
35	30	$324,351	$217,132
40	25	$179,201	$129,818
45	20	$96,838	$75,603
50	15	$50,104	$41,940
55	10	$23,585	$21,037

Table 2: Saving $100 every month at ROI 10% and 12%.

The table is based on consistent and persistent investment on a month to month basis until retirement. In the United States, the average retirement age is 65 years and the calculation in the table is based on someone planning to work till the retirement age. For example, a young professional just starting out at age 25 years will have 40 years of active work life before getting to the retirement age. If this person starts out investing immediately he begin his career, he will have over $5 million dollar in his retirement account if he achieves the 12% annual interest. If on the other hand, his investment returns 10% annually, he will be able to accumulate close to $3 million by the time he turns 65 years. Let's say I am wrong and the market returns is poor that the annual returns are only about 5%, he will still have over a million dollar in his portfolio at retirement. That amount will surely give him some peace in his old age.

Check your age in the chart to estimate what your investment will be worth after certain number of years of persistent investment. The Vanguard has a cool retirement income calculator that you can use to evaluate whether or not you are on track to a financially secured retirement. You will be able to know if you are on track, and you can adjust your saving rate and expected annual returns on your investment. Here is the link to the Vanguard retirement

income calculator website:
https://retirementplans.vanguard.com/VGApp/pe/pubeducation/calculators/RetirementIncomeCalc.jsf

Conclusion

God has endowed the earth with abundant resources. There are so many problems and opportunities in the world today. The money rule highlighted in this eBook is simple, yet so many people ignore the rule. Practice the rules laid out in this eBook and you will soon be on your way to financial prosperity. In life we all have ambitions that we wish to accomplish, righteous desires that we wish to gratify. To bring our ambitions and desires to fulfillment, we need to be successful with money.

This eBook was written to help you win with your finances. You have learned about the money equation and the two variables that you need to know to have surplus at the end of every month. The easiest way to save more money is to reduce your expenses. I have shared fifteen different ways you can achieve that, there are many more options that you can explore. An average person will see a saving of about $100 every month by following these recommendations. The other approach is to find a way of making more money so that your income will always be greater than your expenses.

In part two, I explained seven money principle that will help you to achieve financial prosperity. These principles will help you to learn how to save money, control your expenses, and position yourself for financial prosperity by increasing your ability to earn more money. These are principles that you should practice every month until they become habits for you.

In part three, the concept of dollar cost averaging and compound interest benefits was introduced. This section aimed to teach you how to stay focused and rooted in the market as you set your money aside for investment every month. I shared tabulations that will show you the amount you can accumulate by investing in the market for a long-term horizon.

It is obviously easier for a twenty-five-year-old individual to become a millionaire following this concept than for a fifty-year-old person saving the same amount monthly. This is because the twenty-five-year-old guy has more time to invest and can easily tap into the benefit of compound interest. No matter where you are today, whether you are on track to a great retirement or behind in your goal, following the tips shared in this eBook will help you to save money and boost your savings at retirement.

Finally, there is no need reading a self-help book like this and not following the recommendations. Some of the suggestions in the book will be easier than others, but to achieve result, you must commit to starting the process. Your commitment to the process is what will help you win in the game of money. The ball is now in your court. My advice is that you should play it to your favor.

Now, go win!

www.ingramcontent.com/pod-product-compliance
Lightning Source LLC
Chambersburg PA
CBHW032311240526
45464CB00023BA/2980